ERIC GILL IN OXFORD

Also available from Huxley Scientific Press:

The Oxford Science Walk by Sophie Huxley
Oxford Trees by Sophie Huxley
Darwin's Mysterious Illness by Robert Youngson
Penicillin and Luck by Norman Heatley

ERIC GILL IN OXFORD

S OPHIE HUXLEY

Illustrations by

E DITH GOLLNAST

HUXLEY SCIENTIFIC PRESS
OXFORD

Published by Huxley Scientific Press
35 Marston Street, Oxford OX4 1JU, UK
www.huxleyscientific.com

First published 2011
Text and illustrations © Huxley Scientific Press 2011

ISBN 978-0-9522671-3-3

Typeset in 12/15 pt Perpetua by Ella Hiti and Georgina Mann
Cover design by Geoff Ager
Printed by Holywell Press, Oxford

To the memory of Betty Sandars

Acknowledgements

It is a pleasure to thank the following for their help in the publication of this booklet: Geoff Ager; Fr Brendan Callaghan, SJ; Hannah Dummett; Edmund Gray; Rev. Dr Andrew Gregory; Ella Hiti; George Huxley; Harriet James; Fr Paul King; Lesley Levene; Peter Lewis; Kathleen Lyle; Georgina Mann; Eddie Mizzi; Julian Reid; Rachel Robinson; N. K. Sandars; and Heathcote Williams.

Eric Gill: A Brief Life

Eric Gill (1882–1940) is an important and controversial figure in twentieth-century British arts and crafts. He was a complex man, holding deeply religious views while leading a scandalous private life.

During his lifetime, Gill and his workshop executed and installed many memorials, sculptures, and plaques in Oxford and the county. The work dates from 1904, when Gill was under the influence of the Arts and Crafts Movement, right up to just before his death in 1940, by which time he was well known.

The last chapter of Gill's *Autobiography* is called 'Escapades'. These are the groups of people or ways of thinking that he 'escaped' in order to find his true self: art school in Chichester; architecture in London; the Arts and Crafts Movement; socialism; life in London; and the fine-art world. In the *Autobiography*, he wrote:

> It is thus: we human beings are all in the same difficulty. We are all torn asunder, *all of us*, by this disintegration of our flesh and spirit. And so if in this book I am appearing more spiritual than is credible to some of those I have loved, let them examine their own consciences. I think they will discover, as I have done, that they also are torn asunder and that they also have desired to be made whole.

Eric Gill left school in 1897 to enter Chichester Technical and Art School. Here he learned to draw and letter, but decided that he did not want to become an art teacher. He moved to London in 1900 to train as an architect at W. D. Caröe's practice. He began to attend evening classes in monumental masonry at the Westminster Technical Institute. He also studied writing, calligraphy, and lettering under Edward Johnston – a deep influence on Gill – at the Central School of Arts and Crafts. Soon he began to get commissions in lettering, which he did after work.

By 1903 he felt confident enough to go it alone and left Caröe's office. At this time he was sharing Edward Johnston's lodging in Lincoln's Inn, which had elements of a closed or monastic life that appealed to Gill greatly, as well as ideas of neighbourliness and common practice.

It was Gill who wrote the chapter on letter cutting in Edward Johnston's book *Writing & Illuminating, & Lettering* (1906). Gill had been to Rome and seen the ancient script of 'roman' letters on Trajan's column. He used these letters with elongated serifs in his elegant carving for the Stations of the Cross in Westminster Cathedral. His analysis of these letters was widely used and taught in colleges. Later Gill also designed the lettering for the fascias of W. H. Smith's shops, including one in Paris.

Gill's chapter on letter cutting in Johnston's book, subtitled 'Inscriptions in Stone', is clear and easy to understand. There is not a word wasted or diagram unwanted. He sets out:

> Arrangements – The Three Alphabets – Size & Spacing – The Material – Setting Out – Tools – A Right Use of the Chisel – Incised Letters & Letters in Relief – The Sections of Letters – Working *in situ*.

In 1904 Gill had married Ethel Moore and they set up house in Battersea. His ideas on work practice began to crystallize, and he was involved both with the Arts and Crafts Movement and with the socialism of Ruskin and Morris. The socialism was a reaction initially to the degradation of the Industrial Revolution and its ugliness. The separation of the artist and the workman that had occurred, and which had not been present in medieval times, led to the 'wrongness' of modern practice.

Gill saw the unity of artist and workman combined in one person, and of work being produced by the artist-workman, in one fell swoop. 'The Word became flesh' – the artisan craftsman carves directly on to stone in the way medieval craftsmen did and was thus implementing the reality of Jesus Christ's Incarnation. Jesus was the intermediary between God and Man, and he spoke directly to Man the way Eric Gill sculpted directly on to stone without any intervening medium such as a clay model.

Gill was deeply excited, sexually and artistically, by sculpting. He said of his first female sculpture: 'I was responsible for her very existence and her every form came out of my heart.'

When Ethel was very pregnant with their third child, Joanna, Eric was forced into abstinence. He carved a female form supporting a Greek inscription. Translated as 'there is the sea and who shall drain her dry', this referred to a woman's sexuality and her willing response to a man. Gill felt that with sculpture: 'A new world opened before me… A new alphabet – the Word was made flesh.'

An important early influence on Gill was Ananda Coomaraswamy, who gave a lecture at the Art Workers' Guild on 10 January 1908. Afterwards Gill wrote: 'I believe that no other living writer has written the truth in matters of art and life and religion and piety with such wisdom and understanding.'

Coomaraswamy was half Tamil, half English. After a colonial job in Ceylon, he travelled in India and became enthused by the arts and crafts of the subcontinent, and by Indian spirituality. Back in England he lived near Chipping Campden and, using William Morris's press, he published seminal books on Indian art. Gill was influenced by him because he discussed Man's work and leisure, and also, most importantly, the nature of what is sacred and what is profane.

Coomaraswamy wrote: 'The artist is not a special type of man, but every man is a special kind of artist.' This made a deep impression on Gill. In *The Arts and Crafts of India and Ceylon* (1913), Coomaraswamy says:

> In nearly all Indian art there runs a deep vein of sex-mysticism. Not merely are female forms felt to be equally appropriate with male … but the interplay of all psychic and physical sexual forces is felt in itself to be religious.

Gill couldn't have agreed more. Like Coomaraswamy, he was also a disciple of William Blake, and, like Blake, he believed in social, spiritual, and sexual change and reform.

Gill's first exhibition of sculpture in January 1911 included a mother and child group, and a courtesan, the stone of which was partially painted. The show was a great success. Gill had arrived in the fine-art world – the last of his 'Escapades'. He was to reject London art society and turn to Catholicism and the simple life. It happened quite easily, as if the previous years had made him ready for this.

In 1907 the Gills had moved down to Ditchling in Sussex to find a simpler life away from London. Others followed them: Edward Johnston, the calligrapher and typographer, in 1912 and Hilary Pepler, the printer, writer, and poet, in 1915.

Ethel Gill took to the country life and they soon had farm animals (a cow and a pig and some chickens). These were Ethel's responsibility: farming was women's work; men's work was sculpture and letter cutting. It remained this way for the rest of their lives, essentially a medieval arrangement.

At this time Eric wrote:

> I am doing all sorts of lettering for a living and between times, writing, arguing, preaching, jawing, persuading anybody who cares that good construction is the only thing that can be taught or talked about… From above you'll see that mine is a very simple life and a very simple creed.

Gill had his apprentice Joseph Cribb with him at Ditchling. He carved a 'golden calf' for a nightclub in London. At the same time, Gill was writing to the artist Jacques Raverat about peace and freedom to sculpt in a plain space: 'What is more austere than a chisel and a hammer?' Gill was already marked out by his clothes – a stonemason's smock and square paper hat, combined with red knickerbockers, woollen stockings, and a belt. He looked odd and different.

His charges were initially very modest – in 1901 he asked for one shilling per hour for inscriptions. His work was recorded in his personal diaries, which were written for his information only and contained details of his sexual experiences and family life in addition to his work.

After the 'Escapades', Catholicism seemed to offer certainty and completeness. It was partly a 'kick against the pricks' tendency and partly 'what is the use of art?' For a Catholic, art is for the glory of God and the Word made flesh. 'It is not symbolic,' as a monk in Louvain told Gill that summer of 1912. Gill was impressed by the simple communal living of the monks, and he was thrilled by the plainsong and chanting:

> All unprepared and innocent … I knew infallibly that
> God existed and was a living God – just as I knew in
> the answering smile of a child or in the living words
> of Christ.

On returning to Ditchling, he and Ethel took instruction:

> I became a Catholic because I fell in love with the truth.
> And love is an experience. I saw. I heard. I felt. I tasted.
> I touched. And that is what lovers do.

They were received into the Catholic Church on 22 February 1913. Ethel changed her name to Mary. On Sunday morning they went to Mass and took communion and went walking with Leonard and Virginia Woolf, who lived nearby at Rodmell.

Later they moved house to Ditchling Common. By now they had three daughters: Betty was 8, Petra 7, and Joanna 3. The girls realized that life was a serious business. They were taught by their parents: arithmetic, drawing, Latin, history, and geography by Eric, and 'all domestic accomplishments' by Mary. At this time Gill was working on one of his greatest achievements – the Stations of the Cross for Westminster Cathedral. He commented on the commission:

> I was almost unknown in any respectable circles and,
> I suppose, entirely unknown to Catholic ecclesiastics…
> Had it not been that I was willing to do the job at a price
> no really 'posh' painter or sculptor would look at,
> I should certainly never have got it.

One of Gill's apprentices in the 1930s, David Kindersley, wrote on his technique:

> His attention was remarkable… No tool was ever forced beyond its capacity. All stages were in progress at once over the various parts of the carving, the projections always being a stage ahead, so that, for all the world, it appeared a simple question of removing a series of skins of differently textured stone. Strength and firmness of form were assured not only by the clarity of his vision but in no small degree through his technique.

The Stations remain one of Gill's greatest works. The plain style was in harmony with the plainsong of the cathedral and the plain words of the service:

> Critics always say that I am a person who attempts to be Egyptian or Syrian, or something or other. That is simply not the case. I am working in the only style in which I can work. I am not a learned antiquarian who can work in any style at choice.

As he said, 'I was really the boy for the job.'

Joseph Cribb had joined him in 1906 as an apprentice, and by 1920 the workshop had seven apprentices and assistants. Gill's assistants also cut the commissions but the conception was always Eric's. The skilled stone carvers who were part of the community at Ditchling, and later at Capel-y-ffin and Pigotts, were all experts in the Gill style of lettering. He called them 'chaps', but they called him 'Master'.

Lettering was done in many materials, not just stone. He used marble, cast bronze, engraved brass, painted wood, and copper sheets beaten on the reverse (repoussé work). War memorials and wall tablets were fixed flush with the wall surface to become part of the building. The size of letters varied and changed within one job from roman capitals to lower case to italic, and were painted red and blue or gilded to make them more visible in low light. To make the letters fit a line there is a calligraphic stroke or flourish. His later roman letters were more perfect, but 'absolute equality is quite unnecessary', he said. To quote

Edward Johnston: 'Freedom is an essential quality of all good work.'

Gill designed thirty-eight war memorials. His training in an architectural practice gave him a feel for placing and absorbing a monument into a setting, be it in a town or a church.

In the early 1920s Hilary Pepler and Eric Gill set up St Dominic's Press to print their thoughts and art. Pepler says:

The first thing that struck me as an observer of Gill at work was the sureness and steadiness of his hand at minute detail… When I wanted a tailpiece to end a chapter or an initial letter with which to begin one, he would tumble to the point at once, probably improve on my suggestion, supply the block ready for the press within an hour, and come in to see it printed that same afternoon.

In 1924 Gill quarrelled with Pepler and moved his family and workshop to Capel-y-ffin in the Black Mountains in the border country of Wales. It was very far from anywhere. The artist and writer David Jones stayed with the Gills in Wales for long periods. He became engaged to Petra Gill. The engagement was chaste, and in 1928 Petra broke it off because she wanted a family and felt David was not worldly enough to support her. Jones had a nervous breakdown after a prolific period of painting. He painted Petra, newly married to Denis Tegetmeier, in a picture called 'Petra im Rosenhag'. This was a modern version of the medieval 'Madonna in a Rose Bower'. A Georgian candlestick holds her votive light, and flowers and candles denote a shrine. It is a very beautiful evocation of a mother.

Before her marriage, Petra was being used sexually by her father, as was her older sister, Betty. The hothouse atmosphere of art, Catholicism, sex, and family all thrown together was to characterize the rest of Gill's life. His diary shows his frequent sexual encounters with many women. A special mark was used in the diary to denote sexual intercourse. He had a long-running affair with his sister Maud that continued to his death. Any young girl was seen as fair game. For example, Agnes Cribb had been approached by Gill when she was engaged to the apprentice stonemason Joseph Cribb. As a young man, Gill used prostitutes in London, and soon after he and Mary were married he had an affair with a 'liberated woman'. His incestuous affairs with Petra and Betty produced some wonderful art (Petra naked in the bathtub, for example). These sexual interludes were conducted while Mary and Joanna were shopping in Brecon.

Gill had some uncompromising views on Christianity and sex:

> I wish I could get you to see the point about Xtianity – e.g. when we 'marry' we don't say to a girl: madam you realise what we are is the embodiment of an idea (or do you?). We say: darling, we two persons are now one flesh – or words to that effect. It's a love affair first and last. Joining the Church is not like joining the I.L.P. or the 3rd International. It's like getting married and,

speaking analogically, we are fucked by Christ, and bear children to him – or we don't.

So when we make love, according to Gill, it is a joining in divine love of holy potency (man) with the passivity of the Church (woman). This certainly gave Gill an explanation of his own sexuality which he could combine with his Catholicism. However, the sheer outrageousness of his activities relied on the silence of others, and Gill's status as paterfamilias was never seriously challenged within the community after the quarrel with Hilary Pepler.

Gill becomes ridiculous to us because of the flagrant breaching of his faith's precepts, his eccentricities, and his lifestyle. In 1932 he had a complete breakdown at Pigotts in Buckinghamshire, to where they had all moved in 1928, and Petra found her father wandering across the courtyard with total amnesia. He was taken to hospital and was sufficiently ill to make his confession and take communion. However, he recovered gradually and saw visitors, rejecting those like Pepler who came to make their peace with him. He was interested in the nuns who nursed him, doubtless making some sexual connection with their role. Joanna defied her father to marry René Hague, as Betty had done when she married David Pepler, Hilary Pepler's son. These were grave affronts to the paterfamilias.

His public life (by this time he was becoming famous) and his sexual life were so at odds with one another that they must have caused conflict in his mind. Throughout the diary entries are comments on illicit sexual behaviour such as 'this must stop'. But it didn't stop, it just went on. 'Bath and slept with Gladys' (another of his sisters) is a typical entry. It was too exciting to stop, too interesting, and too good for his creative urges. Other people at Capel-y-ffin and Pigotts kept quiet because of Gill's persona or because of his hold over them. Many people must have known what was going on but did not have enough moral insight into the situation to stop the abuse – for abuse it was.

Shortly after Gill's breakdown, his third daughter, Joanna, married René Hague, who had set up a printing press at Pigotts.

In 1931 Gill had been commissioned by the BBC to do a sculpture on the front of Broadcasting House in central London. 'Ariel and Prospero' was created in 1932 and Gill spent the best part of that year working on it. The sculpture was a great success, Gill saying that the figures of the old man and young boy could be seen as God and His Son.

In 1933 he was commissioned to carve panels for the Archaeological Museum of Palestine in Jerusalem, and went there the next year to execute them.

By 1934 things were getting much more comfortable at Pigotts. Gill accepted an Honorary Associateship of the Royal Institute of British Architects and received a prestigious commission for a large carved relief in the lobby of the Council Chamber of the League of Nations building in Geneva, which brought him international recognition. The central panel is 8 ft × 30 ft in its final form; there are also a left panel representing

Man's gifts to God and a right panel depicting God's gift to Man (the whole of the world). Some of Gill's other works are on a similarly large scale. The New College war memorial has 270 two-inch and 5060 one-inch capital letters. In the next few years he carved a tombstone for G. K. Chesterton, became an Honorary Associate of the Royal Society of British Sculptors, and was elected an associate of the Royal Academy. In 1939 he began his last work, the Stations of the Cross, at St Alban's Church in east Oxford.

In 1940 Eric Gill was diagnosed with lung cancer and died on 17 November. He is buried in Speen Churchyard, near Princes Risborough in the Chilterns. His epitaph reads:

PRAY FOR ME

ERIC GILL

STONE CARVER 1882–1940

AND FOR MY MOST DEAR WIFE,

MARY ETHEL 1878–1961

Works by Eric Gill in Oxford and the Surrounding Area

Balliol College

The passage to the chapel at Balliol has on the left (west) side a seven-panel war memorial in cast bronze. Bronze is usually cast by the lost-wax process, which in this case makes raised, rounded letters. The names and dates are fitted in where space demands it. There are 190 names. It is not easy to read because of the darkness of the passageway.

Inside the antechapel is a very plain bronze memorial plaque to Henry Herbert Asquith, Earl of Oxford & Asquith, 1852–1928. It is immediately to the right of the doors into the main part of the chapel. Inside the chapel, to the right of the communion rail, is a bronze tablet on a marble background to Edward Caird, 1835–1908, Master of Balliol from 1893 to 1907. The inscription has lively spaced roman capital and lower-case letters, followed by five lines of Greek.

Blackfriars

Blackfriars in St Giles is a Dominican convent and a permanent private hall of the University of Oxford. Eric Gill carved the stone above the entrance:

HUNC CONVENTUM ALTERUM
NOVUM EADEM DIE QUA PRISCUS
FUNDATUS EST AD MCCXXI
FRATRES PRAEDICATORES
LONGUM POST EXILIUM REDUCES
POSUERUNT XVIII KAL SEPT MCMXXI

In translation:

This second, new convent, founded on the same day as the old one in AD 1221, *was established by the Preaching Brothers, after a long exile, on the 18th day before the Calends of September 1921.*

In the modern calendar the date is 15 August, the Feast
of the Assumption of the Virgin, the 700th anniversary
of the original foundation by the Dominicans on
15 August 1221. Gill carved this tablet in 1937.

Brasenose College

Above the entrance to the chapel there is a stone
plaque in memory of Albert Watson. This is a very
early commission for Gill (1905), as can be seen by the
shapes and spacing of the letters:

. In memoriam

ALBERTI · WATSON · A · M ·

Socii, Bursarii, Principalis, iterum Socii,

viri litterarum studiis excultissimi.

Sermone inter familiares lepidissimo & ornatissimo,

pari modestia ac sapientia.

Fuit amicis carissimus, nemini non amicus.

Collegii amans,

ET · BENEFACTOR · EXIMIUS ·

Obiit 21 Nov. 1904 Aet. 75

In translation:

> *In memory of Albert Watson, MA, Fellow, Bursar, Principal, and
> a second-time Fellow. He was a man most refined in the study
> of letters. In converse with his associates most elegant and neat,
> he was alike unassuming and wise. He was most dear to his
> friends, and unfriendly to no one. A lover of the college, and an
> outstanding benefactor, he died on 21 November 1904 at the
> age of 75.*

Campion Hall

Campion Hall is a Jesuit foundation whose Master
from 1934 was Father Martin D'Arcy, SJ, who wrote
widely about religion. The current Master thinks that
the works owned by Campion Hall were gifts from
Eric Gill to Father D'Arcy.

In the entrance are two frames holding respectively
seven and nine wood engravings. The group of
seven consists of: three crucifixions; an image of
a lion; a bookplate with the letters JM and JD in
the corners; Christ teaching; and Christ expelling

the moneychangers from the Temple. The group of nine consists of: four images of mother and child; a Christmas scene with an angel blowing a trumpet, two adults carrying a pick and shovel, and some children; Christ in glory; another version of Christ expelling the moneychangers from the Temple; a crucifixion; and a central image of Christ's face similar to that on the Turin Shroud. They are all signed 'Eric Gill' in pencil.

On the Micklem Hall staircase is a wood engraving, signed 'Eric G' and numbered 9/10 (in pencil) of Christ at a table with bread and wine and two disciples with 'AND'

woven in front of them. The block from which the engraving was made was 4½ in × 7 in.

In the coffee room is a wood engraving signed in pencil 'Eric Gill', 4½ in × 4 in, called 'The Mirror' – a fashionable woman tries on a hat with long feathers in front of a large mirror.

On the main staircase, set into the wall, is a bas-relief carved in stone, 18 in × 15½ in, inscribed 'St Martin pray for us'. St Martin, in a First World War helmet and cloak, acknowledges the beggar from his horse. (The horse has wonderful dreadlocks for a mane!) St Martin was a Roman soldier who gave his cloak to a beggar.

Later he was visited in a dream by Jesus, who said that he was the beggar who had asked for the cloak.

Apparently Gill gave the figure of St Martin Father D'Arcy's face, but D'Arcy objected, so Gill made the beggar look like him instead.

In the antechapel is a framed design (9¾ in × 17¾ in) for the lobby of the Council Chamber of the League of Nations building in Geneva. The subject of the central panel of this relief is the Creation of Man by God: *Ad imaginem Dei creavit illum*, or 'God created him in His own image' (Genesis 1.27). Also in the design is a paraphrase from Gerard Manley Hopkins's poem 'The Wreck of the *Deutschland*': 'God mastering me, giver of breath and bread, world's strand sway of the sea, Lord of living and dead, over again I feel thy finger and find thee', where the word 'God' has been substituted for 'Thou' in the original. It depicts Adam reaching out for God's hand. Written in pencil is 'centre panel ½ in scale (½ inch equals 1 foot)' and 'League of Nations, New Buildings, Foyer to Council Chamber, relief carving in Hopton Wood stone. 28′6in Eric G 6 July 1935'. In the bottom left-hand corner is written 'Fr D'Arcy wants this'.

To view the collection of works by Eric Gill at Campion Hall, please write to The Master, Campion Hall, Brewer Street, Oxford OX1 1QS.

Harris Manchester College

At the end of the main corridor near the Bursary there is a bas-relief portrait of Frances Power Cobbe with, below, an early inscription by Eric Gill. Cobbe was a formidable intellectual who was also a journalist, an early feminist, a radical, and a fervent antivivisectionist.

The inscription is on green Connemara marble (Cobbe was from an Irish family) and the lettering shows resemblances to Edward Johnston's scripts of about the same time (1908). Also carved here are butterflies and a shamrock. The bas-relief portrait is by H.R. Hope-Pinker.

Holy Rood Church, Abingdon Road

There are three items of interest in the Church of
Holy Rood. The first is an altarpiece by Anthony
Foster, a pupil of Gill's, in the style of Gill. The piece
shows Christ on the Tree of Life with typical Gill head,
face, and foliage. The main altar has the inscription
DUX VITAE MORTUUS REGNAT VIVUS, which is from
the Easter sequence and means 'The Leader of Life,
having died, reigns in Life.' The lettering is by Kevin
Cribb, son of Laurie Cribb, who had been one of Gill's
apprentices. Kevin Cribb also carved the huge letters
on the massive font with its two curved basins. The
letters are approximately 8 inches high, deeply incised
on the outside of the font, and very impressive.

Merton College

Eric Gill's 'Eternal Flame' monument in Merton
Grove is to Andrew 'Sandy' Irvine, who came up to
Merton College from Shrewsbury School in the Hilary
term of 1922. He was a keen rower and rowed in the

ANDREW
COMYN
IRVINE
1902·1924
PERISHED
NEAR THE
SUMMIT
OF MOUNT
EVEREST
JUNE
1924

Oxford boat in the University Boat Race in 1922 and 1923. It appears to have been during a University expedition to Spitsbergen in the summer of 1923 that he came to the attention of the Everest team. The monument is a three-sided obelisk of Clipsham stone, about 7 feet high, with a sculptured flame.

Andrew Irvine and George Mallory were last seen just below the summit of Everest on 8 June 1924. Mallory's body was discovered in 1999, but Irvine's has yet to be found. If a camera that Irvine had with him is ever discovered, it may be possible to retrieve photographs of the two men. It is not known whether they had reached the summit.

In the antechapel, there is a memorial to Walter How. The inscription reads:

M. S.

WALTERI WYBERGH HOW

HUIS COLLEGII PER XLVIII ANNOS SOCII

VIRI PIETATE, BENEVOLENTIA, IUDICIO INSIGNIS

ANTIQUITATIS INDAGATORIS INDEFESSI

OBIIT ANNO SALUTIS NOSTRAE MCMXXXII

AETATIS SUAE LXXII

SENIORIBUS IUNIORIBUSQUE DESIDERATISSIMUS

In translation:

Sacred to the memory of Walter Wybergh How, a Fellow of this College for 48 years, a man renowned for his piety, goodwill, and judgement, a tireless investigator of antiquity; he died in the year of our salvation 1932 at the age of 72, greatly missed by old and young.

New College

The chapel, antechapel, and adjacent cloisters date from the late fourteenth century. The antechapel is spacious and contains a statue of Lazarus by Jacob Epstein. On the south wall is a large war memorial designed by the architect C. H. Holden, for which Eric Gill was the stonemason. The memorial is in Hopton Wood stone in an unpolished frame with a double-bead and cylinder motif all around. It measures 27 ft × 4½ ft, and the main area that is lettered is made up of three huge slabs of stone. At the top is an inscription in a rounded script of three lines of three-inch capitals, with the carved letters painted in red. It is spaced to fill the line.

> In memory of the men of this college who died serving their country during five years of war 1914–1919 by land, sea / and in the air, in Flanders, in France, in Italy, in Macedonia, in Gallipoli, in Palestine, in Mesopotamia, in all places to / which they were called, men worthy of all they learned here and an example to all those who come after them.

Following this are 228 names in full, painted blue (now faded), in twenty-one lines. The capital letters are about 1½ inches high, on a polished surface. The year dates are gilded. Gill left-justified the lines in his usual way, leaving spaces at the right-hand side. At the foot is a line commemorating various 'Servants of the College'.

Gill carved the memorial in 1921. David Jones (see page 7) visited him in Oxford when he was working on it and painted some of the letters.

RE, The Honourable VICKERS, JAMES KE N, sometime Choristers:

This truly impressive memorial is complemented by a small Hopton Wood tablet nearby on the east wall of the antechapel in memory of the German nationals who had been at New College before the war and who had fought for their country and died in 1914–1919:

> In memory of the men of this college who coming from a / foreign land entered into the inheritance of this place / & returning fought and died for their country in the war 1914–1919.

Following this are the names of three members of the college who were German nationals. The same double-bead and cylinder motif is used. The names are in red,

PRINZ WOLRAD~FRIEDRICH ZU WALDECK~PYRMONT FREIHERR WILHELM VON SELL: ERWIN BEIT VON SPEYER &c.

the inscription is blue. An ampersand is used on this memorial, not 'and' as on the main memorial. The letters are slightly larger than on the big memorial and the stone is polished all over. The architects were Adams, Holden & Pearson and it dates from 1930.

In the cloisters there are three more monuments by Eric Gill. On the left as you turn out of the entrance is a Hopton Wood tablet to the memory of Gilbert Charles Bourne, 1861–1933. The Latin inscription reads:

M.S.

GILBERTI CAROLI BOURNE D. SC., S.R.S

HUISCE COLLEGII OLIM SOCII ET TUTORIS DEINDE

CUM ZOOLOGIAE FACTUS ESSET PROFESSOR COLLEGII

MERTONENSIS IN SOCIETATEM TRANSLATI

QUI UT IN ANIMALIBUS ET INVESTIGANDIS ET EXPLI-

-CANDIS SOLLERS FUIT ET SEDULUS, ITA, SIVE PATRIAE

STRENUUS PROPUGNATOR VEL EXERCEBAT MILI-

-TIAM VEL DOCEBAT, SIVE REMIGIBUS QUORUM IN

ARTE FUIT PRAESTANTISSIMUS CONSILIA PRAEBEBAT

ET EXEMPLUM, OMNIA SEMPER FACIEBAT

PRO VIRIBUS

OBIIT A.D. VIII ID. MART MCMXXXIII NATUS ANNOS LXXI

In translation:

Sacred to the memory of Gilbert Charles Bourne DSc, FRS, formerly Fellow and Tutor of this College, thereafter appointed Professor of Zoology and translated into a Fellowship of Merton College. Expert and diligent in investigating and explaining animals; a doughty champion of his country in the exercise and teaching of military skill; himself outstanding in the art of rowing, an example and an adviser to oarsmen; he used to do everything with all his might. He died on the eighth day before the Ides of March in the year of our Lord 1933 at the age of 71.

The dates are in red and all the lines are of different height. Bourne's name is in red, but the inscription is black. The script is left-justified, 'Pro viribus' is indented, but the line beginning 'Obiit' is left-justified. This is very peculiar compared with the consistency shown elsewhere in Gill's work. It dates from 1933.

Round the corner is a Green Hornton stone (1935) to the memory of the novelist and playwright John Galsworthy, OM, 1867–1933.

The stone is cracked. The six lines of capitals are centred, and painted white with a hand-drawn typeface. The letters differ in height from row to row. The last tablet, to the memory of Sir Henry Erle Richards, KCSI, KC, MA, BCL, 1862–1922, is to the right of the entrance and is of Hopton Wood stone with a delightful tulip decoration. The letters are lower-case and upright and are more like a printer's typeface.

Oxford University Press, Walton Street

In 1931 Gill was commissioned to carve and gild an
oak tablet for the Record Room of Oxford University
Press. It reads:

THIS ROOM, FORMERLY THE OFFICE OF THE BIBLE
PRINTERS OF THE UNIVERSITY, HAS BEEN FURNISHED
AS THE RECORD ROOM OF THE PRINTING HOUSE BY THE
GIFT OF CONSTANCE MEADE, GREAT GRANDDAUGHTER
OF BISHOP PERCY OF DROMORE, WHO IN HIS OWN DAY
CONTRIBUTED TO THE LEARNING OF THIS PRESS.

The Playhouse, Beaumont Street

The very plain inscription 'PLAYHOUSE', gilded, is
above the porches on the front of the theatre, facing
the Ashmolean Museum. It dates from 1938.

Radcliffe Science Library

Above the doorway facing South Parks Road in four-
inch letters is the inscription 'RADCLIFFE LIBRARY' and
three coats of arms. Inside the library, outside the old
rare books room, are two sliding oak doors with six

bas-relief panels with portraits and initials of Roger Bacon, William Harvey, Robert Boyle, Christopher Wren, Robert Hooke, and Johann Jacob Dillenius.

Bacon is depicted with his book *Opus Maius*, Harvey with a heart, Boyle with his air pump, Hooke with a microscope, Wren with St Paul's and a telescope, and Dillenius with a sunflower. Each panel is carved separately out of one piece of oak and set in the door. The panels are carved on both sides, but the backs are not so detailed. Inside the room are two angels on either side of a clock, holding a scythe and rake respectively. This work dates from 1933.

Rycote Chapel, Thame

There is a 13 in × 30 in Hopton Wood stone tablet in the chapel commemorating Alfred St George Hamersley, KC, JP, and MP for Woodstock from 1910 to 1918, 'who lived at Rycote 1911–1929 and preserved this chapel'. Signed EG at request of Miss C. Hamersley, 1930. Rycote Chapel is owned by English Heritage and is not always open to the public.

St Alban's Church, Charles Street

The foundation stone of the building, designed
by T. Lawrence Dale, was laid on St Alban's Day
(22 June) in 1928 and the church was consecrated
on 1 May 1933. Eric Gill's Stations of the Cross were
installed between 1938 and 1945. They are the only
Gill Stations in an Anglican church. The Stations
are incised with a V-cut, on polished Hopton Wood
stone. The incisions are coloured red or blue. Gill
finished the drawings three weeks before his death
in 1940. Nine of the Stations were carved by him,
the remaining five by his workshop. Gill priced the
Stations at £25 each.

Each Station has figures in flowing robes, in graceful
yet moving poses. Below each Station is a line of
description taken from the Gospels. Station VII has
a soldier in a tin hat (the Second World War was
breaking out at the time of carving). Station VI shows
St Veronica holding a cloth to wipe Jesus' face (this
story is from a medieval source); Jesus falling for the
first, second, and third time (Stations III, VII, and IX)

also do not appear in the Gospels. In Station XII Jesus dies on the cross. St John holds a scroll with the Greek inscription 'ΑΓΑΠΑΤΕ·Μ‹Ε›' ('love me', from John 14.15). 'INRI' – Iesus Nazarenus Rex Iudaeorum (Jesus of Nazareth, King of the Jews) – is nailed to the cross above Jesus' head. In Station VIII, the three women are Mary mother of Jesus, her sister Mary, wife of Clopas, and Mary Magdalene. Jesus speaking to his mother can be found in John 19.26 and the 'daughters of Jerusalem' are mentioned in Luke 23.28–31.

St John's College

Above the inner entrance to St John's College, in the tower, is a statue by Eric Gill of John the Baptist, holding a staff (1936; see page 28).

The sculpture 'Tobias and Sara' (18½ in × 23 in × 4½ in), owned by the President and Fellows of St John's College, was begun by Gill on 4 September 1926. He initially called it 'Lovers with Arms Round Necks' and carved quickly to finish it on the afternoon of 15 September. Tobias and Sara are two figures from

the Book of Tobit in the Apocrypha. Tobit sends his son Tobias to recover a debt in the company of someone who turns out to be the angel Raphael, who rescues Sara from the demon Asmodaeus. Sara is described as 'sensible, brave and very beautiful' (Tobit 6.12). Certainly this sculpture shows human love at its most tender and sensitive. It is a beautiful thing.

The sculpture, which was said to have been done by
Gill 'for himself', was donated to the college in 1988
by Brian Roberts. It has recently been cleaned and it
is displayed on a windowsill in the college library. The
Librarian can be approached if one wishes to view.

St Mary's Church, Garsington

This memorial to Lady Ottoline Morrell in Hopton
Wood stone, originally carved in 1939 for her daughter
Julian, is now in St Mary's Church, Garsington, near
Oxford.

There is an exquisite profile of Lady Ottoline, with
a classical ribboned hairstyle, looking very wistful. On
either side of the bas-relief are Doric pilasters.

Ottoline Morrell was a great influence on
twentieth-century art and literature in Britain. She
was married to Philip Morrell of the Oxford brewing
family, and they shared an interest in art and liberal
politics. Theirs was an open marriage: she had affairs
with the philosopher Bertrand Russell and the painter
Augustus John, among others.

The Morrells lived at 44 Bedford Square in Bloomsbury and at Garsington Manor in Oxfordshire, where they welcomed many guests, including Stanley Spencer, Mark Gertler, and Dora Carrington. The Morrells were pacifists during the First World War and took in conscientious objectors, such as Duncan Grant, Clive Bell, and Lytton Strachey, as well as those recovering from the battle front, like Siegfried Sassoon.

Ottoline was also a great supporter of the Bloomsbury Group, and hostess to W. B. Yeats, L. P. Hartley, T. S. Eliot, and Aldous Huxley, who lampooned her in *Crome Yellow*. She may have been the inspiration for Lady Chatterley, and also appears in Alan Bennett's *Forty Years On*. There are portraits of her by Duncan Grant and Augustus John.

St Thomas More Chapel, Foxcombe Road, Boar's Hill

The chapel is in the garden of a house on Boar's Hill. It is very simple, with white walls. The altar is from Gill's private chapel at Pigotts, near High Wycombe,

as is the tabernacle behind it. The altar is at hip height and rests on two hexagonal white limestone pillars. The top is of beautiful polished dark grey stone with darker inclusions and is cool to the touch. The slab is 50 in × 26 in × 2 in. The tabernacle has a limestone pillar, approximately 5 feet high, which broadens out into a large rectangular form with a gold-painted door in wood. This opens into a gilded chamber 6 in × 8 in × 6 in, which holds the chalice and wafers. The extreme simplicity of these objects is very much in keeping with the chapel itself.

Canon Crozier, who built Holy Rood, in Abingdon Road, was a friend of Mary Gill's and this is how these two pieces came to be here at St Thomas More. The priest in charge of Holy Rood can give permission to visit the St Thomas More Chapel.

South Park, Headington Hill

South Park, to the south of Headington Hill, was sold by the Morrell family to the Oxford Preservation Trust in 1932. In 1959 the park was given to the city so that it could be an amenity for all. A massive monolith at the bottom of the park, adjacent to the road, has Eric Gill lettering recording the assistance of the Pilgrim Trust and David and Joanna Randall-MacIver. The 12-foot-high stone monolith dates from 1935. The lettering is large and can be read from the road. There are twelve lines, centred with V-cut lettering in a smooth panel, the rest of the stone being rough.

University College

Low down on the west wall of the antechapel there is a slate plaque. The inscription reads:

> In memory of ANDRE JOHN
> MESNARD MELLY .A.M,M.C.,M.A.
> B.M., Comm.nr of the College 1919–1922
> Leader of the British Red Cross Unit
> in Abyssinia, who died at Addis Ababa
> of a wound received when rescuing
> a wounded Abyssinian, May 5th 1936
> Aged 37. BEATI MISERICORDES

Gill has spaced the words to fill the rectangular stone completely. The punctuation on this memorial is somewhat eccentric.

, who died at Addis Ababa
of a wound received when rescuing
a wounded Abyssinian,

Wolvercote Cemetery

One of the best tombstones in Wolvercote Cemetery is one by Gill commemorating Eleanor Constance Lodge, DLitt, CBE, 1869–1936. She was Vice-Principal of Lady Margaret Hall and Principal of Westfield College, London. The italic inscription reads:

With thee is the fountain of life
In thy light we shall see light.

Wolvercote Community Orchard

The wall opposite the Trout Inn at Godstow contains a stone cut by Eric Gill to mark the purchase of land by the Oxford Preservation Trust in 1934. The land, now the site of the Wolvercote Community Orchard, was a gift from Philip Leslie Agnew, who bought it in memory of his son Ewan Siegfried Agnew, who was an undergraduate at New College just before the First World War. The plaque was installed in 1940.

Bibliography

Gill, Eric, *An Essay on Typography*, Sheed & Ward, 1931.

Gill, Eric, *Autobiography*, Jonathan Cape, 1940.

Gill, Evan, and Peace, David (eds.), *Eric Gill: The Inscriptions*, Herbert Press, 1994.

MacCarthy, Fiona, *Eric Gill*, Faber & Faber, 1989.

Skelton, Christopher (ed.), *Eric Gill: The Engravings*, Herbert Press, 1990.

Yorke, Malcolm, *Eric Gill: Man of Flesh and Spirit*, Constable, 1989.

Notes

The Oxford colleges are usually open to the general public for a few hours each day. It is best to telephone beforehand. St John's College Library should be visited by prior arrangement, as should Campion Hall (see page 14). Visitors to University College should obtain permission from the Porter's Lodge.

The present whereabouts of the oak tablet carved by Gill for Oxford University Press, which is described on page 20, is unknown.

John the Baptist at St John's College